The Hawaiian Shirt

The Hawaiian Shirt

Its Art and History

by H. Thomas Steele

ABBEVILLE PRESS • PUBLISHERS • NEW YORK

Dedicated to the people of Hawaii, their spirit of ''aloha,''
and to my wife Fiona

Library of Congress Cataloging in Publication Data

Steele, H. Thomas.
  The Hawaiian shirt.

  1. Aloha shirts—Collectors and collecting. I. Title.
NK4890.S45S74 1984   687'.115   83-73422
ISBN 0-89659-419-X

Editor: Walton Rawls
Design and principal photography by H. Thomas Steele

Table of Contents

Introduction

As someone active in the graphic arts, I have always appreciated the fabric design of the Hawaiian shirt and have been cataloging its variety for more than ten years. The functional use of creative colors and the amazing artistic renderings in these shirts certainly capture the simplicity and spirit of Hawaii. Although the Hawaiian language contains only 12 letters in its alphabet, the Islands' visual vocabulary has been virtually unlimited. Furthermore, the innocence with which Hawaiians formerly translated their life and heritage onto fabric ranks these shirts with the finest of American folk art. Their old-guard designers considered integrity toward their work a factor as essential as technique, and this most certainly is a lost art form.

Technology and mass-production have rendered obsolete the artistry and individuality there once was.

This book is not merely an encyclopedia of Hawaiian design. It is a portrait of a special time and place, both real and imagined, of the place's history and geography, and of the spirit of its people as seen in its wearable art.

Hawaii is still an alluring paradise. Today, the local shops carry plenty of tropical garments, but the original silk, rayon, or cotton shirts are not to be found. Most of what is offered now shares the identical, mass-produced, synthetic prints made for every member of the family. You know you are in Hawaii when her *muu-muu* matches his shirt!

—H. Thomas Steele

ABOVE: *The Latter Day Saints Aloha Centennial, 1850–1950, is celebrated on fabric with any and all Hawaiian motifs; 5-color silkscreen on rayon, 1950.*

The kings and queens of Hawaii were featured
on this spectacular shirt—King Kamehameha, King Kalakaua, and
Queen Liliuokalani drawn in a more realistic vein than
on most Hawaiian shirts; rayon, mid-1940s.

Prints of Paradise

"ALOHA" is the Hawaiian word that extends the warmth, friendliness, and pride of the Hawaiian people to their islands' visitors. It is difficult to imagine that clothing could capture the essence of a word, but the Hawaiian shirt truly symbolizes aloha spirit to islanders and visitors alike. In July of 1936, a shirtmaker named Ellery J. Chun coined the term "Aloha Shirt," an apt characterization for such an eloquent garment. He was the first to make the shirt on a commercial basis—through Wong's Products, which previously had manufactured work clothes. The shirts sold for as little as a dollar in Chun's own King-Smith store.

Originally, both Western missionaries and early American pioneers had brought the styles of the "civilized" world to the inhabitants of the Hawaiian Islands. Many of the pioneers traveling the Oregon and the Overland trails to California wore a type of garment called the "Thousand Mile Shirt"—so named for its durability through months of hard travel and grimy work. This shirt was worn outside the trousers and usually had a decided pattern of color. Even then there was regular contact between California and Honolulu because sailing ships heading round Cape Horn tacked out into the ocean to get favorable winds to and from various Pacific ports. The "Thousand Mile Shirt" found its way to the Islands, and the Chinese immigrants took to wearing it. In due time, so did the Hawaiians.

The earliest foreign settlers in the Hawaiian Islands were the Chinese

ABOVE: *Close-up of Island couple in tropical moonlight; 1940s.*

and Japanese. They brought with them their myriad talents and trades, among them the art of tailoring. It was the Oriental seamstresses who copied the humble dress of the Western missionaries. They also made the solid-colored work shirt worn by the early Hawaiian plantation laborers; known as the *palaka*, it was to become the forerunner of the more casual aloha shirt. The missionaries did their part by insisting on clothing the natives' nakedness. They set about teaching the women to construct everyday gowns guaranteed to fit even the fattest. Two words of direction in running the seams, *holo* (go) and *ku* (stop), were repeated so often that the women named their new dress the *holoku*,

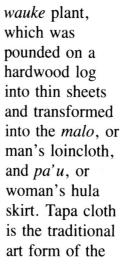

which became the *muu-muu*.

The early shirts utilized traditional Polynesian designs, the most notable being motifs from *tapa* cloth. Tapa, or bark cloth, was made from the pulpy inner bark of the *wauke* plant, which was pounded on a hardwood log into thin sheets and transformed into the *malo*, or man's loincloth, and *pa'u*, or woman's hula skirt. Tapa cloth is the traditional art form of the South Pacific islands. Its sheer beauty of color and decoration, its texture and durability made Hawaiian tapa of old supreme. This fabric was worn for protection against weather as well as for work, and it was used in the most sacred ceremonial rites marking birth, death,

ABOVE: *Early 1900s* tapa *cloth design on bark; forerunner of the Hawaiian shirt.*

marriage, war, worship, and tribute. The motifs were produced by hand-painting or stenciling of designs left by the impressions that were hand-carved on blocks of wood. The coupling of brilliant hues was a characteristic of the original tapa designs, but the prints were colored with natural vegetable dyes that faded quickly and mellowed with age to ocher and brown earth-tones. The colors themselves were significant— yellow was designated for victory, red for valor, white for holiness, and so on. The original patterns from paradise were more geometric and less floral than the contemporary Hawaiian counterparts.

Silk and cotton were predominantly the materials used in the early 1920s and '30s, but it was difficult to register the dye patterns on silk during early attempts at mass-production. The DuPont Company solved that problem in 1924 when "rayon" was introduced to the world. Rayon was a synthetic product manufactured from the cellulose fiber of natural wood pulp; it held the dyes and felt silkier than silk itself. Furthermore, it was more durable and extremely inexpensive to produce. The demise of this particular quality and blend of rayon ended with a fire at the DuPont factory in the early 1950s.

Developments in the late 1920s had turned Hawaiian shirt production into a viable business. Amid gala celebrations, the elegant Royal Hawaiian Hotel on Waikiki Beach was opened officially, and with that event tourism came to Hawaii via

ABOVE: *Fluid* lei *pattern floats around this shirt from the '40s.*

the cruise ships. Because tourists sought exotic souvenirs of their visit to a tropical paradise, small local shops began producing custom-tailored versions of the much sought-after Hawaiian shirt for the visitors and the American servicemen stationed there.

Although local companies were making garments in quantity, the bulk of the production was still work clothes. In 1921 Wong's Products was mass-producing the *palaka*. However, it was the small tailors, such as Musa-Shiya The Shirtmaker of Shoten, Ltd., and designer Elsie Das of Elsie Das's Hawaiian Originals, who pioneered the Hawaiian shirt as we know it. Within only a short time, Hawaii's plentiful natural assets inspired local designers to custom-make prints exclusively for Hawaiian families, whether for social status or some special occasion such as a wedding. Clothing soon became a veritable canvas for palm trees, tropical jungles, beaches, volcanoes, Hawaiian legend, and recent history. Hawaii's garment industry began to flourish because sportswear was a year-round business. The clothing manufacturing business is still Hawaii's third largest export to some of the most fashionable cities in the world.

These early shirts were not readily accepted by the islanders themselves, but the first Hawaiian Products Week in 1930 helped advertise and popularize island-made garments among local residents.

In the mid-1930s, the growing number of visits by tourists, as well

ABOVE: *Matson liner* Lurline *coming into port, tourists disembarking and receiving* leis; *coconut buttons, postwar 1940s.*

as United States Army and Navy personnel stationed in Hawaii, increased the souvenir market. To meet this demand, two companies underwent a transition from tailor-made to factory-made production of sportswear. In 1936, Kamehameha Garment Company, Ltd., founded by Herbert and Millie Briner, and Branfleet (later Kahala), founded by George Brangier and Nat Norfleet, were the first to incorporate. Sportswear produced by these companies exhibited remarkable skill in the blending of island motifs and exciting color combinations with quality craftsmanship. Today, collectors consider these early shirts to be some of the most desirable. In that period the fabric generally was designed in Hawaii, printed in California, and sent back to Hawaii to be manufactured into shirts. Kamehameha and Branfleet were set up to supply the sportswear market on the mainland, but during the Christmas season of 1936 a shipping strike stranded fabric in California and finished garments in Hawaii. The garments were put on sale locally, but the results were not what they might have been. By 1939 the industry had made up for lost time by toting up a half-million dollars in export sales alone, and hundreds of small companies jumped on the bandwagon.

Two of the most popular prints of the time were the "shell tapa" Polynesian design and the "aloha tapa," the latter designed and printed by Virginia Thompson of California Handblock in Hermosa

ABOVE: *Wildly colored novelty shirt promoted the Royal Hawaiian Band, Matson Lines, and a* luau *at Don the Beachcomber; postwar 1940s.*

Beach, California. Upon first glance the "aloha tapa" looked like a simple tapa print, but under closer scrutiny the word "aloha" could be found designed into the pattern. Kahala, whose firm the shirt was designed for, did not even realize this for at least five years.

These two prints were modified only slightly during the fourteen years they were in use. While Kamehameha offered the flashier, brighter designs, Kahala introduced the "pineapple tweeds," an extremely popular shirt style in the mid-1930s. The material looked like hand-woven linen but in fact was made from fabric remnants scooped up from the milliner's floor. The shirt came in plain, solid colors, with long sleeves and an open collar. The fabric was so durable that

Chrysler wanted to use it to upholster automobile seats. The only graphic element was the Royal Hawaiian Crest with the motto, "The life of the land is perpetuated in righteousness." Famous Hawaiian Duke Kahanamoku helped popularize this shirt and was given a fifty-cents-per-dozen royalty by Kahala. Later, Kahanamoku signed with a New York company named Cisco and carried its line to prominence.

The years from 1936 to 1939 were an impressive growth period for the garment industry as well as the Hawaiian economy. Many small businesses opened up, hoping to claim their share of the profits. With each company introducing at least fifteen new designs a year, there were literally thousands from

ABOVE: *The* kahili, *or royal feather standard, crowns this shirt and was used ceremonially; late 1940s.*

which buyers could choose. Shirts with blue or black backgrounds seemed to be greatly in vogue—so much so that at times strollers in the Royal Hawaiian Hotel lobby looked as if they were wearing tropical uniforms. Men's shirts accounted for over fifty percent of the sportswear sold. While men bought shirts with figures on them, women chiefly purchased floral designs.

World War II may have called a halt to sportswear production, but it also drew attention to the Hawaiian Islands. Hawaii had long been a stopover point between Guam and the mainland, and thousands of servicemen streamed into the military installations on Oahu. After the war tourism escalated, for Pearl Harbor and Hawaii were part of the American vocabulary. The garment industry was bursting at the seams due to postwar expansion, and "What Hawaii makes, makes Hawaii" became the industry's motto. The Hawaiian Visitors Bureau joined forces with transportation businesses such as Matson Liner Navigation Company and United Air Lines to encourage tourism and trade. Hawaii became Vacationland. Shirt manufacturers added the magic words "Made in Hawaii" to their labels to stimulate sales and it worked—just as "Made in Hollywood" did for films. The shirts grew wilder and the market was flooded. A strong sense of color had emerged after the war in reaction to years of drab military uniforms and wartime clothing worn

ABOVE: *In 1951, United Air Lines sponsored a "Hiway to Hawaii" promotion.*

in the States. Although tourists needed time to get accustomed to these showy shirts, they were soon sporting the fanciest patterns available—only to find upon returning home that those tropical prints did not fit easily into their suburban environments. Nothing but a neighborhood luau or a return trip to Hawaii could bring the shirts out of mothballs.

In 1948 Aloha Week was initiated in Hawaii, and this celebration permitted even staid businessmen to wear Hawaiian shirts to work during that period. It was a huge success, and this custom is still observed today. In fact, businessmen in Honolulu wear Hawaiian shirts every Friday.

A strong Far Eastern influence in the design of Hawaiian shirts developed after the war. Because labor costs were still low in Japan, many Hawaiian-based companies had their garments manufactured there and, occasionally, even designed and printed.

The 1950s saw continued postwar expansion. Sportswear became acceptable not only on the beach but as full daytime and evening wear. In addition to myriad Hawaiian companies, mainland imitators, recognizing a good thing when they saw it, began to manufacture "Hawaiian" sportswear. The movement generally cheapened the product, lowered the demand, and hurt prices. There were exceptions. Alfred Shaheen's company, for example, specialized in handprinting techniques that authentically duplicated the ancient tapa designs. His line of clothing was constructed by a team of craftsmen,

ABOVE: *Tourist attractions—hula girls, outrigger canoes, and surfers—were featured; silkscreen on rayon, coconut buttons, early 1940s.*

including designers, stylists, and printers. In 1957, recognition was given to garments judged most outstanding by the Hawaiian Fashion Guild. Kahala placed first, followed by Paradise Sportswear, Kamehameha, and Shaheen.

Hawaii's push for statehood added fuel to the sagging fashion industry's fire. Vying for annexation at the same time was Alaska. Some fabric was designed showing Hawaii as the 49th state, but in reality it became the 50th in 1959.

Hawaiian fashion went international, leaving the spirit of local design far behind. It became less definitive of Hawaii and more worldly. New York and Japan spawned new designers to keep up with huge yardage runs, and shirts lost their exclusivity as thousands of designs were produced each year. The imagery became standardized as the highly mechanized yet economical technique of roller printing replaced the hand-powered silk-screen. The innocence was gone. Because of this mechanization the patterns produced were the smaller repetitive ones. Gone were the large, intricately correlated patterns with an overall design. But shirts and sportswear continued to sell in volume. With the resurgence of surfing in the 1950s, the garment industry again experienced an upward swing that continued through the 1960s and '70s and now into the '80'.

The true Hawaiian shirt is from another era. Every detail, from the fabric itself to the finished

ABOVE: *The irony was Hawaii's presumption that it would become the 49th state; politics caused Alaska to beat Hawaii to statehood by three months; rayon, 1955.*

This beautifully rendered version of a Hawaiian maiden
had decidedly Western features, detailed on this back panel.
The front's only color was the left pocket; long-sleeved, 1950s.

product, exhibits quality handcrafted work and aloha spirit. The garments manufactured in Hawaii were always much sought-after because each article was sewn individually, and seams were double-stitched for durability. Special inks and brilliant dyes, raw silk and quality rayon, and dazzling patterns, designs, and illustrations of every tropical motif imaginable were integrated to produce these works of art. Connoisseurs of the Hawaiian shirt look for collectible particulars: rare designs and color combinations; original labels intact to help determine when and where the shirt was made; the type of material used; matched pockets that do not interrupt the fabric's pattern; two-flapped pockets worn for more formal occasions; buttons made of kopra seeds, coconut shells (produced as early as 1940 and still being used today), or metal emblazoned with the Royal Hawaiian Crest; long-sleeved versions meant for evening wear; signed or dated shirts; and, finally, the shirt's condition. Some of the dyes used tended to deteriorate the fabric more quickly than others. Yellow was the most stringent of the dyes and was mainly used in smaller areas of the shirt design. Rayon, being a natural fiber, has a certain lifespan to it and will eventually decompose. It won't last forever, unlike the incorruptible polyester of today. Appreciate the old shirts and feast your eyes. They don't make them like they used to!

ABOVE: *Feather capes were worn by kings and warriors ceremonially and in battle; cape designs represented certain virtues of the wearer; coconut buttons, 1939.*

Luscious anthuriums sweep out of their frames on this
state-of-the-art shirt, showing the care taken in
design, printing, and construction, with matched pocket
and wooden buttons; crepe-de-chine, 1939.

Hollywood Hawaiian

HOLLYWOOD was greatly instrumental in popularizing Hawaiian fashions to a worldwide audience. The appeal of the Hawaiian image was exuded often in Hollywood productions, ranging from Dorothy Lamour's sarongs to Elvis Presley's shirts in his popular movie *Blue Hawaii*, and its best-selling record. Bob Hope and Bing Crosby traveled the tropical trail more than once in their "Road To . . ." film series. Bing was a big proponent of Hawaiian shirts and brought many of them back to the States after his first visit to Hawaii. Ginger Rogers had seductive gowns made from Hawaiian fabric, while pin-up Betty Grable posed for a studio publicity photo, for her 1942 movie *Song of the Islands*, wearing a sexy Hawaiian-styled bathing suit. Montgomery Clift, Burt Lancaster, Ernest Borgnine, and Frank Sinatra sported Hawaiian shirts made by the Cisco Company in the 1954 movie *From Here to Eternity*. Clift died in a beautiful one at the end of that famous movie. Even political celebrities such as Harry Truman and Dwight Eisenhower gave magazines cause to write articles about their leisure-time tropical wardrobes. Arthur Godfrey strummed his ukelele, sang of the Islands' magic, and looked quite casual while wearing his colorful shirts on television. Island fever spread with the advent of television and the popularity of the beach and surfing movies of the 1950s and '60s.

ABOVE: *Dorothy Lamour graces her record cover of Hawaiian songs from* Rainbow Island *in a sexy sarong; 1944.*

LSP-2426

LIVING STEREO

A ''New Orthophonic'' High Fidelity Recording

RCA VICTOR

PRESENTS
AN ORIGINAL SOUND TRACK ALBUM
14 GREAT SONGS

SEE
ELVIS
IN HAL WALLIS'

Blue
Hawaii

14 GREAT SONGS

Elvis was immortalized and glamorized on this soundtrack
album cover from his film *Blue Hawaii* in 1963. The flawless
photograph was a well-propped studio set-up, complete with
rear-projected background and facial retouching.

Montgomery Clift and Donna Reed are shown in scenes from
the 1954 movie *From Here to Eternity*. Set in Hawaii
of 1941, the male cast was costumed in magnificent Hawaiian
shirts made by the Cisco Company.

On this 1951 cover of *Life*, Harry Truman appears in
his ''seashore shirt with seagulls.'' Vacations gave him a
chance to show off louder aspects of his large and
controversial wardrobe.

LEFT: Arthur Godfrey entertained the public via television with his warm smile, wild shirts, and whimsical ukelele, 1955.

RIGHT: Betty Grable shows off those famous legs and more in an attractive Hawaiian swimsuit from the '40s.

© Twentieth-Century Fox

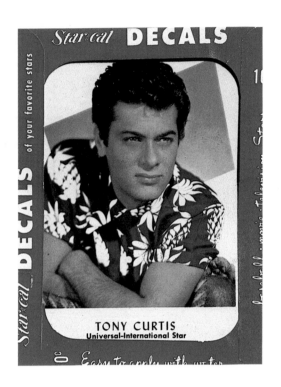

LEFT: Ann Sheridan poses comfortably in her pantsuit with complementary Hawaiian shirt; 1948.

RIGHT: Tony Curtis strikes a "candid" pose in one of the most popular shirts of the time; 1940s.

ABOVE: Ida Lupino reclines on a chaise for photographer George Hurrell in a 1941 *Esquire* datebook.

LEFT: Paulette Goddard was voted ''Sensation Girl of 1941'' in this international fan magazine portrait.

ABOVE: In the 1943 movie, *White Savage*, Jon Hall sports the breadfruit motif while Maria Montez models a strapless floral dress.

RIGHT: Bing Crosby set his own style— his trademarked porkpie hat, pipe, and Hawaiian shirt; shown here with writer Carroll Carroll and producer Bob Brewster, 1944.

FOLLOWING SPREAD: *Hand-colored postcard backdrop shows majestic Diamond Head from Waikiki, 1915. Shown left to right: The pink Royal Hawaiian Hotel nestled in Honolulu; Island chain with exploding volcanoes through bamboo; surfing and the Aloha Tower; coconut flower and seeds; map and royalty; net fishermen and surfers surrounded by flowers and ukes.*

Patterned Shirts

THE designs and imagery of hibiscus, ukeleles, and leis prevalent in the patterned shirts were so popular that garment manufacturers employed innovative means to supply the demand. While maintaining the basic print, they simply changed the background tints, allowing customers a choice of favorite color combinations. The more popular the print in any series of these shirts, the more numerous the color changes. For example, the hibiscus pattern was produced in as many as twelve different color variations. The reason this was practical was inherent in the silk-screen process of fabric printing itself. One color was printed at a time and each successive color was registered to the previous one, giving the craftsman much latitude in color selection and application. Although the prints looked like brightly colored wallpaper, their designs were well thought out. Allover patterns that were made to repeat themselves on the long bolts of fabric were the work of the designer himself and not a computer, which does that task today. Borrowed heavily from the immediate environment, the motifs on most of the shirts that fall into this category are floral and bought by both males and females because the many color treatments were a satisfactory selection for both sexes. There was a certain positive image to negative space ratio that was aesthetically pleasing to the eye in these patterned shirts. Depending on the design, there was always a proper size to use the image on the shirt, and these shirts did it well.

ABOVE: *Ukelele and floral motif inspired by early cruise ship menu covers; 1939.*

TOP ROW: Traditional ukelele and *lei* pattern was a perennial
favorite and came in a variety of colored backgrounds; rayon, 1940.

BOTTOM ROW: Strikingly beautiful birds-of-paradise pattern
showed that light and dark backgrounds worked easily with minor
color alterations; two-flapped pockets, rayon, 1940s.

TOP ROW: Bunches of bananas wove a busy pattern around flowers
and fronds on these two renditions; late 1940s.

BOTTOM ROW: The classic hibiscus pattern sold well to both men
and women with a myriad of colors to choose from; postwar 1940s.

TOP ROW: Thatched huts and '50s netting created a swirl of
movement on these contrasting shirts; rayon, 1950s.

BOTTOM ROW: The Royal Hawaiian crest and torch ginger
flower combined to create an intricate pattern; late 1940s.

TOP ROW: Pali Hawaiian shirts used rayon with a sheen
not unlike that of silk, with traditional Island flora; 1940s.

BOTTOM ROW: *Kihi-kihi*, seahorses, and seaweed formed a popular
pattern in the early 1950s.

This lively pattern did not come from the ''less-is-more''
school of fabric design, but it works well, incorporating hula girls
and their lovely hula hands, hibiscus flowers, and
the Royal Hawaiian crest; coconut buttons, 1938.

Shirt Labels

HAWAIIAN shirt labels often proved to be as fascinating and unique as the shirts on which they were sewn. It is possible to date some shirts accurately by knowing the companies and studying the subtle changes in their label design. The sportswear manufacturers selected logos and names indicative of Hawaii—Paradise Sportswear, chosen to promote the romance of the Islands, and Kamehameha Garments, named after a past king, are two examples. Famous local landmarks, palm trees, Hawaiian phrases, tropical fish, surf-riders, fishermen, and hula girls were typical trademarks. Labels bearing the information ''Made in Hawaii'' and ''Made in California'' (California's mystique was as valid as Hawaii's) proved to be big sales-boosters. A close-up view of these labels shows that even the smallest detail was handled artistically, for they are a subtle form of advertising. A good shirt brought business if the buyer knew who made it and was reminded of where it was bought. It also worked in reverse: if a designer's name was on it, the merchandise had better be good. People were as fashion conscious then as they are today. They still buy clothes by the label.

ABOVE: *The Aloha label named an entire industry and guaranteed the authenticity of the garment; 1936.*

The labels shown are some of the originals that
pioneered top-of-the-line versions of sportswear. Labels
intact help date and add worth to garments.

Diamond Head, Hawaiian phrases, and Honolulu added
the tropical touch needed for that special image of
paradise. Sales increased based on that lure.

California labels worked as well for sales as did
Hawaiian ones, but the predominant motif here seemed to
be palm trees, no matter what coast they came from.

Duke Kahanamoku

DUKE Paoa Kahana-moku was the embodiment of Hawaii's friendliness and true aloha spirit. Pure Hawaiian and the descendant of *alii* (royalty), he became Hawaii's international ambassador of good will and its Official Greeter. He served nine consecutive terms as sheriff of Honolulu. He, more than any other celebrity, popularized Hawaiian shirts among both Hawaiians and mainlanders. As an Olympic gold-medal swimmer of four Olympiads and a champion surfer (a member of the Surfing Hall of Fame), Duke went to Hollywood in 1925 where he was typecast as a native tribal chief. He appeared in such films as *Wake of the Red Witch* with John Wayne and *Mr. Roberts* with Henry Fonda. Duke's name on a Hawaiian shirt warranted its authenticity, and it also assured a tremendous increase in sales for the companies whose product he vigorously endorsed. He was associated with Kahala Sportswear (Branfleet) as a fashion consultant in the mid-1930s and then with the New York-based Cisco Company in 1949. His death in 1968 saddened the people of Hawaii who loved him. Catalina Sportswear now carries the Kahanamoku name on one of their shirt lines. His name is also perpetuated in Hawaii's annual Duke Kahanamoku World Surfing Championships on Oahu.

ABOVE: *Duke with his old board; the* Hui Nala *emblem is that of the first surfing club in existence.*

The stylized sea fan shirt made by Cisco came in
numerous single colors on heavyweight rayon; late 1940s.
INSET: Duke, wearing a long-sleeved version of the
shirt described, posed with Richard Boone and Peter Lawford
in Waikiki, 1947. Lawford's ''Malibu'' board was made
of balsa and fiberglassed.

TOP ROW: Linear palm trees graced these shirts designed in
New York for Duke's label; rayon, 1950s.
BOTTOM ROW: Extensive use of negative space added drama to
the floral poinciana-patterned border shirts; 1950s.

This painterly pattern of marlin fishing and
flamingos was inspired by Florida, but sold in Hawaii
on Duke's *Champion* label; 1950s.

PHOTO AT RIGHT: *Duke in the 1930s, coming in after
bodysurfing at Makapuu.*

43

TOP LEFT: Pineapples, orchids, and trumpet vines were utilized
in this border print; 1950s. RIGHT: Rows of palms
created the vertical look in three colors on rayon; 1950s.

BOTTOM LEFT: Two-pocketed shirt with hula dancers perched
on lively leaves; long-sleeved, late 1940s. RIGHT: Pineapples
and their cross-section were pictured on this
Cisco shirt; late 1940s.

An entire Hawaiian village was depicted, complete
with grass huts, spearfishing, outrigger canoes, and the
ever-present coconut palm; early 1950s.

FOLLOWING SPREAD: *Pineapple postcard background photographed
in Wahiawa, Oahu, 1910. Shown: Six versions of pineapple
patterns, from the simple to the complex, were put onto
fabric proudly displaying Hawaii's main export. The shirt
at far right was the largest selling shirt of all time.*

Border Shirts

PROBABLY the most artistic and striking of the Hawaiian shirts are the border shirts. Certainly the most collectible and visually pleasing group, they were a garment-industry luxury by today's standards, for a great deal of fabric was sacrificed in their construction. Designs were specifically created to take into account all the particular areas on a shirt. They were cut a bit longer than the other types of shirts in order to feature their handsome designs, which were either centered in the middle of the front and back sections or worked to the seams. Subordinate designs were also worked to the sides or around the bottom, thus suggesting the name-tag border shirts. Some prints never repeat themselves within the same shirt.

Most all of them have a linear quality that is vertically oriented. The more collectible shirts have patterns that match along the front plackets, the pockets, the side seams, and even the collar, so that the design is not interrupted. More than one-third of the material normally used in a shirt gets wasted in making a border shirt, but even more is lost if the patterns are to be matched perfectly. The designs had to be very well thought out, which was not easy considering that the stencils were cut by hand directly on the silkscreen—a rectangular, two-dimensional surface. With all this in mind, the manufacturers still produced these artistic creations with little concern for cost or waste. Warning: it is a sacrilege to tuck in a border shirt!

ABOVE: *One of Champion's best, the design extended from top to bottom in a most graphic way; 1940s.*

Pikake, fish, vanda orchids, and island flowers of
all sorts create vertical trails of engaging patterns on
silk-screened rayon; 1940s.

Night-blooming cereus, coconut palms, torch ginger,
and a maze of shells were elements culled from the local
environment; matched pockets, 1940s.

This rare shirt captured the drama of indigenous
anthuriums in rich airbrushed tones by Kamehameha Garments;
crepe-de-chine, wooden buttons, 1936.

Familiar floral motifs shown in new combinations
of color and design. Note how this source of the art
was abstracted; rayon, 1940s.

Matched pockets continued this stylized design uninterruptedly
up the front and sides. Birds-of-paradise and pink ladies
were the flowers used; coconut buttons, 1940s.

Picture Shirts

PICTURE shirts were a unique breed. They involved the use of actual photographs that were adapted to the photo-silkscreening process. Today there are mechanized methods of achieving a similar effect photographically through light-sensitive emulsions on fabric, but the earlier shirts were hand-screened by highly skilled craftsmen. Because full-color process printing was costly and the possibility existed that misregistering of the colors could ruin entire bolts of fabric, many mass-produced picture shirts were one-color photo prints in blue, red, brown, or green. The full-color shirts that were produced, with their airbrushed sunsets and radiant palm trees, are suggestive of collages and remain some of the most appealing offshoots of aloha shirts ever produced. They featured depictions of Hawaiian points of interest, including Diamond Head, the Aloha Tower, and the Royal Hawaiian Hotel in all its pinkness, or personalities such as the Coconut Boy, the Hibiscus Lady, and the net fishermen. Instead of sending a postcard while on vacation or taking a snapshot of some prominent sight, the tourists could wear their photo albums home. Shirts picturing scenes of note in California, Florida, and New York were also produced in this process. They caught on in the States following the lead of the sales success in Hawaii, and due to the innovation and the ability to faithfully reproduce famous sights and tourist attractions on fabric.

ABOVE: *Full-color example of a picture shirt with Hawaiian clichés photographed instead of drawn; late 1930s.*

TOP: Detail of Hibiscus Lady showing process of photosilkscreen
on rayon fabric; 1940s.

BOTTOM LEFT: The Florida backdrop detailed skiers, divers,
fishing, and enigmatic flamingos; 1940s. RIGHT: Eliminating black
in the printing yielded less contrast and detail but
gave subtlety to tones not normally associated with
this variety; late 1930s.

This set of monochromatic prints highlights points
of world interest: Crossroads of the Pacific, Diamond Head,
San Francisco cable cars, the Egyptian Sphinx, and the
Hollywood Bowl; rayon, late 1930s-40s.

Classic images are collaged in this group:
coconut tree climbing, hula girls with ukeleles, and the
statue of King Kamehameha; late 1930s.

Matching single-color beach ensemble, and a not-so-subtle
full-color picture tie to dress it up; 1940s.

By today's technological standards it is amazing that the
silkscreeners could hold the registry of color at all on this close-up view.
Note screen's dot pattern and multicolor overlap; late 1930s.

The Designers

AS the demand for custom-made shirts grew in the mid-1930s, designers began to spring up everywhere. Mainland representatives came to the Islands to buy Hawaiian designs because designers outside the Territory could not quite capture what was achieved there. Women far outnumbered male designers of that era, and men handled the business end of the industry. Some designers gained world renown for their fabric creations; others remained anonymous. In 1936, Watumull's commissioned Elsie Das to design a series of fifteen Hawaiian designs in color on raw silk. From then on, hand-blocked silk became her trademark. A feeling of motion also was an integral part of her work. One time, her designs were mistakenly printed onto satin, but Ginger Rogers, Janet Gaynor, and other stars eagerly bought the bolts of cloth and had them made into seductive gowns. The result was an epidemic of inferior work from other designers but an increase in national exposure.

This award-winning designer revolutionized summer clothes and placed Hawaiian designs in the public eye. Some of the other women designers were Elsie Krassas, who studied under Das, Millie Briner of Kamehameha Garments, Betty Gregory of Branfleet, Ethyl Wheeler of Oahu Garment Company, Frances Delpech for McInerney's, and Virginia Thompson of California Handblock.

As a commercial artist with a fine arts background, Eugene Savage

ABOVE: *Fabric translation of Eugene Savage's colorful menu covers; coconut buttons, 1940s.*

A fashion model sports vintage clothing in this calendar pose.

TOP: Muralist Eugene Savage painted ancient Hawaiian scenes; this one dramatizes "aloha" in one gesture—a gift of a flower *lei* to a princely visitor.

BOTTOM: Island feasts, or *luaus*, signaled such high points of life as births, marriages, victories. Roast pig and other delicacies left no one hungry; 1940s.

TOP: Pomp and circumstance marked the monarch's court as his subjects engaged
in hula dancing, sports and games, feasting, and merry-making; 1940s.

BOTTOM: The art and sport of the *hukilau* was a community festival. This mural depicted
a plentiful catch fit for a king as he offered thanksgiving to the gods of the sea.

specialized in painting vivid scenes of Hawaiian history and legend. He was commissioned in the 1930s and '40s to create what were to become award-winning menu covers for the Matson Liners that carried tourists across the Pacific. A muralist at heart, Savage depicted Captain Cook's discovery of the Islands and a luau with King Kame-hameha. His paintings inspired other Hawaiian designers such as

Frank MacIntosh. Their designs were transferred to shirts and dresses that were sold in Hawaii and in shops on board the cruise ships. Savage's murals still can be seen in the Matson Navigation building in San Francisco and are part of the Smithsonian Institution's permanent collection. John Meigs, on the other hand, who worked under the name of Keoni of Hawaii, went from being a textile designer to a

ABOVE: *MacIntosh menu cover was given to passengers on final night of Matson cruise.* RIGHT: *His illustration of a* luau *was used throughout the 1930s and '40s.*

renowned muralist. His widest artistic acclaim came from his Gauguin designs, which were based on woodcuts made by the famous artist in Tahiti. Mass-production might have destroyed the artistic integrity of Meigs's original tapa prints had it not been for the efforts of Alfred Shaheen, who insisted that his company use handprinting techniques to preserve the ancient tapa designs he recaptured. Ellery Chun, Isami Doi, Jerry Chong, Chang Chung, Nobuji Yoshida, George Brangier of Kahala, and Milt Martin of Koret of California were among the more famous of the early creators. Today the tradition continues with Dave Rochlen of Surfline Hawaii, Sheri Holt of Sunshine Hawaii, Gunther Von Hamm, Nat Norfleet, Reyn Spooner, Tori-Richards, Ross Sutherland, Dano and Hoffman of California, Reminiscence, Hang Ten, and Ocean Pacific in the States.

ABOVE: *MacIntosh illustrations translated to fabric.*
They were sold in shops on board the luxury liners steaming
to and from Hawaii; 1940s.

Local garment companies utilized the previous menu
covers and restated them to emerge as new designs, such as
this ''Land of Aloha''; crepe, coconut buttons, 1939.

Kamehameha Garments acquired the rights to use Savage's
murals. Of special interest is the signature of Eugene Savage
found on the inside opening of some shirts; 1937.

Millie and Herb Briner's influence on shirt design
can be seen in this primary-colored border print by their
company Kamehameha Garments; rayon, 1939.

John Meig's homage to the artist Gaugin is evidenced
in this Polynesian print also manufactured by Kamehameha;
silk-screened on rayon, 1938.

Women's Clothing

THE most outstanding Hawaiian fashion for women in long and short lengths was the muu-muu. Introduced to the Islanders by the missionaries, the muu-muu started out as a loose house dress. It covered up what women did not want to be seen. The artistry of local designers combined and created variations of this dress in the form of the *pake muu*, the *holomu*, and the *holoku*. In contrast to the casual loose-fitting type of muu-muu, the pake muu had wing-effect sleeves, full-length body, and was popular as a hostess gown for informal entertainment at home. The holomu, a fitted garment with off-the-shoulder and ruffle collar, was ideal for evening wear. The lovely, fitted holoku was a full-length dress with Hawaiian print that was the essence of feminity for formal affairs. The cut of the early women's shirts, influenced by Chinese styles, led to their being called "tea-timers." The short mandarin-type collar, sleeveless arms, and tailored bodice accented the female figure, whereas the men's shirts seemed too blousy for women at that time. Today, that does not appear to be the case, as women's wear borrows more and more from men's styles.

Although many standard Hawaiian shirt prints were utilized for these women's shirts, many new designs were drawn up specifically for them, most noticeably by Kamehameha and Watumull's. The special designs tended to be more floral than figurative, featuring ginger blossoms, papayas, and orchids as well as the fragrant plumeria, the hibiscus and stylized birds-of-paradise.

ABOVE: *Sleeveless "tea-timer" cataloged all forms of ginger; featured two pockets near bottom, 1940s.*

This set of "tea-timers" essentially employed the
same designs as men's shirts, which showed the universality
of the patterns; 1940s.

The stunning *pake muu* was an adaptation of
the *holoku*, distinguished by a high Chinese collar and
wing-effect sleeves; rayon, 1940s.

Another eye-catching *pake muu* printed by
Kamehameha and produced by Shaheen; popular as a
hostess gown for evening affairs; rayon, 1940s.

Two casual ''tea-timers'' and a sarong dress, a short
dress with a draped skirt inspired by a Tahitian design,
shown with bolero jacket; late 1940s.

The border design worked wonders in new applications, as
evidenced in this fitted sundress; postwar 1940s.

Made in Japan

THE phrase "Made in Japan" formerly carried the connotation of an inferior copy of the original. Whether that idea arose out of jealousy, frustration, prejudice, or cultural differences, World War II certainly had something to do with it. The reality was that Japan could manufacture and produce quality garments for less than Hawaiian-made goods cost, a fact that still holds true today. Japanese influence in shirt production became particularly evident in the late 1940s, although silk and rayon materials were being imported from Japan as early as the 1920s. Production accelerated after the war, and fabric designs began to change. Traditional motifs were being substituted for by tigers, eagles, and dragons; Diamond Head was replaced by Mount Fuji. Among the major department stores, the J.C. Penney chain laid claim to the Japanese-produced Hawaiian garments during the 1950s. You could not argue with the economics.

The price was right, the rayon was of fair quality, but overall the fabric designs suffered due to America's preoccupation with the future—the atomic age, new technology, quantity versus quality. It was a hybrid product that lacked the essence of the original. Hawaii was a melting pot of cultures, and the postwar designs reflected the changes. Nevertheless, a debt of gratitude is owed to that same melting pot, which contributed to the development of the aloha shirt in the beginning. Today, their fabric printing offers fine quality that America now copies.

ABOVE: *Japanese lanterns and bamboo sticks adorn this Oriental pattern; rayon, 1940s.*

Outstanding workmanship not only in the design and printing,
but also in the construction (note perfectly matched pocket) made
this early shirt collectible; crepe-de-chine, 1937.

TOP LEFT: Chinese lanterns housing Hawaiian events showed
the cultural melting pot. RIGHT: The crane as a Far Eastern
symbol appeared with palm trees and brush strokes; 1940s.

BOTTOM LEFT: The only Oriental part of this shirt
was Grauman's Chinese Theatre. Note also scenic Los Angeles
freeway system. RIGHT: Penney's shirt with bridges,
birds, and rushing water; 1950s.

The sacred eagle is transfixed on a bonsai branch in
this shirt produced by Kilohana, meaning ''the choicest tapa'';
crepe-de-chine, 1940s.

Chinese and Japanese cultural elements are denoted
in the designs of this set of garments, as the postwar years
reflected the influx of incoming talent; 1940s.

The towering inspiration of Mount Fuji and graceful Japanese
pagodas contained in Oriental shapes proved that
another coast besides California was interested in Hawaii.

FOLLOWING SPREAD: *The Waikiki Aquarium in Honolulu serves
as the background (still standing today), circa 1920.
Shown: Shirts that envisioned the undersea life of the*
kihi-kihi, *the most colorful fish in the water, and the
peculiar* malolo, *or flying fish.*

Hawaiiana

HAWAIIANA includes shirts that display and celebrate things inherently Hawaiian, be they fact or fiction, legend or lore. Hawaiians are a delightfully proud people whose tale can be told in the illustrations on the shirts themselves. Shirts entreating statehood, honoring once-reigning monarchs, showing maps of the Island chain, and acclaiming the Queen of Aloha Week reflect past and recent history. Hawaii's history is Hawaii's heritage, rich in cultural flavors. Surfers, beachboys, lei ladies, and outrigger canoes are woven into busy patterns, which radiate a gratifying sense of joy and humor. There is a cartoon quality to some of these shirts, which is evident nowhere else in the history of the garment industry throughout the world. The Hawaiians just do not take things too seriously and they know how to laugh at themselves. Some of the floral prints shown in this book are undeniably breathtaking and utilize similar techniques, but the subject matter of the Hawaiiana prints lends the designs a more comic air.

All the clichés are at work: hula girls greeting fully dressed tourists with leis upon arrival, Diamond Head seen in the moonlight to a ukelele serenade, and so on. These images are Hawaii's best propaganda. No need to advertise in expensive travel brochures, the shirts translate the same feeling—namely, that Hawaii is a place of leisure, a place to vacation, a place to relax. Leave your troubles and cares at home. Do something you would rather do. Wouldn't you rather be riding a mule on Molokai?

ABOVE: *Fully-clad tourists leaving gangplank of streamer-strewn* Lurline; *postwar 1940s.*

The Aloha Queen ruled over festivities of Aloha Week,
which began in 1948. She wears the *holoku*, a formal gown
with a train, for this special occasion; rayon.

TOP LEFT: Rare use of the negative-detailed sexy silhouette and hibiscus. RIGHT: Island chain map and Royal Crest float in busy background; 1940s.

BOTTOM LEFT: Surfriders were sporadically interspersed between graphic waves. RIGHT: Human footprints and nonhuman tracks walk side by side in this humorous shirt; 1940s.

The postcard shirt represented well-known motifs of
the time—surfers, hula girls, scenic views, and postmarks of
the cities Hilo, Hana, and Lihue; rayon, postwar 1940s.

TOP LEFT: Island activities at full swing. RIGHT: Floral script
spelling ''Aloha Hawaii'' and pineapple views; 1940s.

BOTTOM LEFT: Cleverly designed fabric juxtaposing airplanes with
ancient customs. RIGHT: Surfboard shirt; early 1950s.

Outstanding five-color pattern of banana trees, hula
girls, and ukeleled beach boys that only repeats itself twice
on the entire shirt; rayon, 1940s.

Examples of the joy of sports and outdoor activities
are a good showing of the cross-section of designs and color
combinations of the early 1950s.

Although the pockets were not matched, this shirt permitted
the viewer to see just how painterly the silk-screen
process could become. Montgomery Clift died in this shirt
at the end of *From Here to Eternity*; late 1940s.

TOP LEFT: Different aspects of the *menehune* legend (leprechauns of Kauai) woven into a cohesive design. RIGHT: Only silk shirt included with any vibrant color; earliest example of mass-produced shirt; by Kahala, 1936.

BOTTOM LEFT: Sugar cane, another large industry, is exhibited in this shirt. RIGHT: Romantic scenes of courting couples reinstate the lure of paradise; late 1940s.

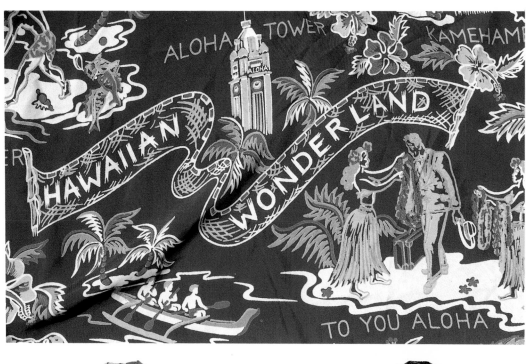

TOP: Detail of wonderful fabric portraying linen-suited
tourist with suitcase being given his proverbial *lei*.

BOTTOM LEFT: The cock-eyed mayor of Kaunakakai and riding
mules on Molokai appear on this novelty fabric. RIGHT: The
Hawaii Druggists Convention created a strange brew and a secret
formula of unknown molecules, probably aspirin; 1950s.

Aloha!

Courtesy of O.K. Harris Works of Art; photo: Eric Pollitzer

ABOVE: *This life-sized sculpture by artist Duane Hanson,
entitled* Tourists *(1971), depicts Mr. and Mrs. America on vacation,
staring at some sightseer's dream.*

Skillfully hidden among the flower *leis* is the ineffable
Hawaiian maiden, and to the sides is the word ''aloha'' written
vertically; made by Kilohana, postwar 1940s.

Acknowledgments

Special thanks to collectors Jerry and Susan Brownstein of The Junk Store, L.A., for my Hawaiian eye; Bill and Jean Gold of Repeat Performance, L.A.; Karl Holm and Michael Alvidrez of Paleeze, L.A.; Diane Candoli and Harold of Harold's Place, L.A.; David Taylor of David's of Hawaii; Ronn Ronck for his information and help beyond the call of duty; the Lichtgarns and Eve for her early wordsmithing; Vince Bantinelli; Russell Morris; Ron Kleyweeg and Daryl Hazen; Jeff Speilberg; Millie Briner and Richard Goodwin of Kamehameha Garments, Honolulu; Jerry Panza of Hawaii's Visitors Bureau; Gage Illo of Catalina Menswear, L.A.; Charles Regal of Matson Lines, S.F.; Alfred Shaheen and Mrs. Matook of Shaheen's, L.A.; Virginia Thompson; George Brangier; Anne O'Neill, Brad Benedict, and Emma Lila Fundaburk for her extensive studies on ''The Garment Manufacturing Industry of Hawaii''; Tony Hoffman; Craig Stanman; Rebecca Keeley; John Kehe; Merrily Kane; Sarah Jane Freymann; Walton Rawls and Philip Grushkin at Abbeville Press; and to my family, friends, and the collectors who made this project a reality— thank God!

''Halakahiki Magritte''
© 1984 SteeleWorks

96